Horned
Frog Care

Photo Credits

M. Bacon: 1, 4, 6, 26, 45, 51, 53, 56 (top)
R. D. Bartlett: 9, 11, 14, 16, 28, 56 (bottom)
Allen Both: 3, 12, 13, 18, 23, 27, 29, 30, 56, 58
Paul Freed: 8, 38, 59 (center)
Jerry R. Loll: 24, 35, 40, 42
Erik Loza: 31

W. P. Mara: 55, 59 (top)
Sean McKeown: 41
G. & C. Merker: 20
Aaron Norman: 5
M. Panzella: 59 (bottom)
Mark Smith: 57, 62
Marc Staniszewski: 7, 15, 33, 36, 43
K. H. Switak: 17, 21, 47, 48, 60

Quick & Easy Horned Frog Care

Project Team
Editor: Tom Mazorlig
Copy Editor: Carl Schutt
Design: Patricia Escabi
Series Design: Mary Ann Kahn

T.F.H. Publications
President/CEO: Glen S. Axelrod
Executive Vice President: Mark E. Johnson
Publisher: Christopher T. Reggio
Production Manager: Kathy Bontz

T.F.H. Publications, Inc.
One TFH Plaza
Third and Union Avenues
Neptune City, NJ 07753

Library of Congress Cataloging-in-Publication Data
Both, Allen.
Quick and easy horned frog care / Allen Both.
p. cm.
Includes index.
ISBN 0-7938-1018-3 (alk. paper)
1.   Horned frogs as pets. I. Title.

SF459.F83B68 2005
639.3'787--dc22
2005004682

This book has been published with the intent to provide accurate and authoritative information in regard to the subject matter within. While every precaution has been taken in preparation of this book, the author and publisher expressly disclaim responsibility for any errors, omissions, or adverse effects arising from the use or application of the information contained herein. The techniques and suggestions are used at the reader's discretion and are not to be considered a substitute for veterinary care. If you suspect a medical problem, consult your veterinarian.

The Leader in Responsible Animal Care for Over 50 Years!™
www.tfhpublications.com

Table
of Contents

What Is a Horned Frog?

Horned frogs, or Pacman frogs as they are most commonly known in the pet trade, can be found in almost any pet store around the country. These frogs go by several names: Pacman frogs, Argentine horned frogs, and Bell's horned frogs. They are all the same large, robust frog, which makes quite an impressive pet. They are called horned frogs because the upper eyelid forms a point above each eye that resembles a horn. The name Pacman frog refers to a video game of the same title that became widely popular in the 1980s. It featured a large, round, yellow character—basically just a giant head—whose goal was to consume everything on the board. People in the pet industry began to call Argentine horned frogs Pacman frogs in the late '80s because of their huge appetite and interest in eating everything they come in contact with, much like the character in the game. Also, large horned frogs resemble a head with legs.

Natural Range

Argentine horned frogs originally were imported from the Chacoan and Pampean regions of Argentina. Ornate horned frogs originate from tropical rainforests in Northern Argentina, Uruguay, and some parts of Brazil.

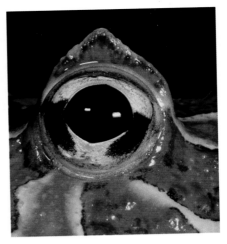

Horned frogs get their common name from the spiky protrusion above their eyelids. The protrusions are not hard or sharp like a true horn.

Chacoan horned frogs originate from the Chacoan regions of South America. The Pampean region (often called the Pampas) receives some rain throughout the year and is in contrast to the Chacoan region that has clearly defined dry and rainy seasons. Although the ornate horned frog is mostly from the Pampean region where there is only slight seasonal change, they tend to be more active during the rainy summer months when they emerge for breeding. Even though the seasonal changes are very subtle, these frogs mostly remain dormant during the

Two Horned Frogs

There are several species of horned frogs that are sold in pet stores and at reptile shows. The two most common are the ornate Pacman frog, *Ceratophrys ornata*, and the Chacoan Pacman frog, *Ceratophrys cranwelli*, which also has an albino form. Other species are occasionally available, but ornate and Chacoan horned frogs are the most readily available.

Quick & Easy Horned Frog Care

Herp Is the Word

Throughout this book, you will see the term *herps*. This word refers both to reptiles and amphibians and comes from the word *herpetology*, which is the study of these two groups of animals. When speaking of the hobby of keeping reptiles and amphibians, you can call it the *herp hobby*. *Herpetoculture* is the keeping and breeding of reptiles and amphibians. A *herper* is someone who participates in the herp hobby or herpetoculture.

These terms are handy to know, not just for reading this book, but because you will see them in other herp publications and the Internet and hear other hobbyists use them as well.

cooler fall and winter months. Of the horned frogs, the ornate is found furthest away from the equator and experiences the coolest temperatures, making it much more tolerant of lower temperatures.

During fall and winter months—or whenever conditions become unsuitable—Pacman frogs remain buried in the ground. In the wild, Argentine horned frogs go through a process known as estivation. This is sort of a hibernation period in which the frog will retain skin instead of shedding it. The skin will build up a protective coating over the frog, sealing in

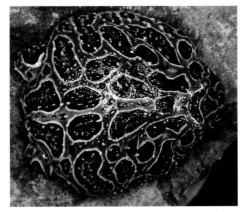

Ornate horned frogs are among the most beautiful frogs a hobbyist can keep, as shown by this large male.

moisture and keeping the frog moist until the summer comes. This sort of cocoon that the frogs build around themselves resembles a plastic coating. The process of estivation is a normal one, and if this happens to your frog, do not be alarmed. The most common cause of estivation in captivity is seasonal change. Lower temperatures and/or a drop in humidity will sometimes stimulate the frog to estivate. If you are keeping the frog just as a pet and aren't planning to breed horned frogs, be sure to maintain warm temperatures and moist conditions year-round to prevent your frog from estivating. During this period the frog will continue to breathe by absorbing oxygen through his skin instead of breathing normally through his nostrils. If the frog looks normal do not bother him at this time, just be sure to always have clean water available for your pet. When temperatures change and the frog is ready, the skin will soften and then shed. After this, the frog's appetite should return to normal and estivation should be concluded for the season. If your frog is estivating because you let the cage get to dry, gradually raise the humidity over the course of a few days by moistening the substrate. This will bring your frog out of his torpor.

Description

Today, these frogs are no longer imported from South America, but rather they are captive bred in large numbers. Thanks to selective

Estivating horned frogs cocoon themselves in shed skin and mucus to conserve moisture. When the rains resume, the skin softens, and the frogs emerge to breed.

Quick & Easy Horned Frog Care

breeding, Pacman frogs are offered in many patterns and colors. The ornate horned frog will typically be a medium to dark green frog with red patches on the back. I have personally seen baby frogs (often called froglets) with bodies that are 80 percent red and have main-

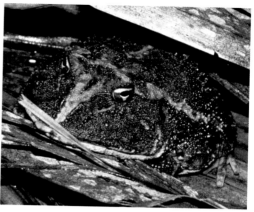

Wild-caught Chacoan horned frogs generally are not as colorful as their captive-bred kin. This wild-caught female is rather drably colored.

tained this color to adulthood. With this much color and personality, it is no wonder why these frogs make such popular pets. The ornate horned frogs also seem to reach larger adult sizes than the Chacoan ones do; however, the ultimate size of these frogs somewhat depends on the size of the parent frogs that produced the babies. Larger adults tend to yield larger offspring; smaller adults tend to produce smaller offspring. Ornate horned frogs can reach a size of five to six inches for adult females and slightly smaller for males. Adult males can be distinguished by loose skin and dark

Frog Superstitions

Argentine horned frogs, or *ezcuerzos* as they are sometimes called by the native people of South America, are creatures of much superstition. *Ezcuerzos* is a Spanish term for toad. People of Argentina and several of the Indian tribes of South America tend to leave frogs and toads unharmed. Frogs are often called *shechu,* or protective spirits of the water. They are also believed to be embodied souls that have been captured by sorcerers.

Scientific Names

You may have noticed that sometimes there are strange looking words in italics that appear after the name of an animal. This is the scientific name, and each animal only has one scientific name. Biologists determine the scientific name of each animal based on what other animals it is related to. The first part of the name is called the genus; the second part is the species. This combination of genus and species is unique for each animal.

The reason we have scientific names is so that scientists all over the world can talk about each animal without worrying about language barriers or other similar animals being confused with the one they want to discuss.

If you use the genus name once, you can abbreviate it to the first letter when you write about it later. So, when I first mention the ornate horned frog, *Ceratophrys ornata*, I have to use both names, but later on I could just type *C. ornata*.

Scientific names may be confusing and hard to pronounce at first, but they actually do make things easier. If you decide to do more reading about keeping pet reptiles and amphibians, you should become accustomed to scientific names, since hobbyists use them frequently.

coloration on the underside of their chin. Males will vocalize in breeding season. Some say their call sounds deep and throaty and resembles the mooing that a cow makes. The Chacoan horned frog tends to remain a bit smaller than the ornate, reaching an adult size of four to five inches. Once again, the females are larger than the males. Sexing is done in the same fashion as the ornate horned frog. You can find these frogs in brown, bright green, and sometimes oranges and yellows. There are also commonly available albino genetic mutations of these frogs. All of these can become quite impressive adults.

Quick & Easy Horned Frog Care

Whether you choose an ornate horned frog or a Chacoan one, you will get an interesting and fairly easy to care for pet. Most pet stores carry these colorful, hardy, and intriguing frogs. If you are a dedicated pet owner, caring for these frogs is not a difficult task.

Big Mouths

Having the name Pacman frog and the voracious appetite to go along with it, it should be no surprise that these frogs can bite. This is not to make you afraid of owning one, but to warn you to be careful. Horned frogs will show aggression if they feel threatened. In my experience, these frogs are less aggressive now than when first introduced into the hobby. This is possibly due to captive breeding of the species, calming down their natural instincts. Nonetheless, your frog will bite if he feels threatened or if he thinks you are food. Because they work under the assumption that anything moving should be eaten, they will sometimes mistake a finger for food and give you a bite. If this happens do not struggle, and the frog will quickly let go. Pulling your finger away will probably result in a worse injury as your frog will try to hold onto the

The Chacoan horned frog is the only horned frog that has an albino form, although it is certainly possible that albinos will be discovered in the other species.

What Is a Horned Frog?

struggling "prey." If the frog does not let go, try running cold water over him. The water should cause the frog to release his grip.

Selection

When picking out a frog for a pet, make sure to choose one who looks alert and has clear eyes and skin. Cloudy eyes or

The defensive stance of the horned frogs involves standing up tall, puffing up their bodies, and gaping—all attempts to look bigger and more fierce.

skin could signal a problem. Make sure the frog is strong and tries to jump away if disturbed. Be sure to pick a plump little frog, not one with his hips sticking out. Be aware of the animal's cage conditions. Make sure the water and cage are clean. If the frog seems happy and healthy and the sales people seem knowledgeable, you should be off to a good start with your Pacman frog.

Most pet stores today have adequate ways of transporting the animal

Ornate horned frogs generally sport some red in their coloration. They tend to be more spherical than the Chacoan horned frog.

home. Usually, your frog will be sent home in a deli cup with holes punched in it or possibly a small plastic carrier. Purchase your frog when you have decided it is right for you to get one, and only after you have already prepared the proper environment for your new pet. This holds true for any reptile or amphibian pet. If you are reading this book before acquiring one, you are on the right track.

Housing Your Horned Frog

Caring for a horned frog is not too difficult. They do not need much space or equipment. However, there are some particulars that you will have to provide if you want your horned frog to thrive. Creating the proper environment for your new frog is essential to ensure a healthy, long, happy life for your new pet. Remember that, in captivity, your frog is totally dependant on you to provide him with the right food and environment. Providing less than adequate housing is inhumane.

Choosing a Cage

The first step toward ensuring your frog has a healthy life is to pick out a proper enclosure. Choosing a cage that will

The common horned frogs, like this ornate, get quite large. However, they are inactive animals that do not require a lot of space.

accommodate the frog for his entire life is best. A 10-gallon aquarium will be an ideal size to house the frog even when fully grown, for even large horned frogs do not need much space. They are fairly inactive animals. If you want to provide a larger cage, you may certainly do so. However, a smaller cage will only suit a juvenile.

Although horned frogs do not jump or climb, it is always a good idea to use a screen cover to keep out the family cat or unsuspecting fingers of houseguests. A screen top with locks or clamps is best to ensure no unwanted intrusion into the cage.

Other commercially made cages are available that will also be adequate to house your horned frog. When choosing a cage, be sure to pick something that holds water. As with any amphibian, being able to maintain water and humidity within the cage is essential. Also, remember to choose an enclosure that is durable and easy to maneuver for cleaning. Maintaining a clean healthy environment is important, so make sure the cage is easy to drain and rinse.

Housing Juvenile Frogs
Setting Up the Terrarium

How you set up the terrarium depends on the size and age of the frog. We will start by discussing housing for froglets. Several different substrates can be used for juvenile Pacman frogs. Paper towels, sphagnum moss, or compressed coconut husk beddings are easy to clean and will keep an adequate level of humidity for a baby frog. Paper towel is a simple substrate for horned frogs, but it needs to be replaced daily. In most cases, the frogs make a mess of the towel trying to bury themselves in it and end up exposing the bottom of the cage. Sphagnum moss is another option for substrate and in most cases will work well. The moss should be rinsed at least once a week and replaced at least once a month. This substrate provides a more aesthetically pleasing look. The last substrate I will mention is a coconut husk bedding. This bedding is typically sold

as a compressed block, and when soaked, it expands into a fluffy bedding that maintains humidity well. Once again, more pleasing to the eye than paper towels and fairly easy to care for, the coconut husk bedding should also be changed twice a month.

A shallow water bowl should be provided so the frog can climb in and hydrate himself when needed. Remember that horned frogs are not strong swimmers, so the bowl should be shallow and allow the frog to enter and exit easily. Attractive water bowls are now

Deli cups lined with paper towels can serve as a simple but adequate setup for rearing juvenile horned frogs. This saves considerable time if you are keeping a number of frogs.

easy to come by at most pet retailers. The water should be changed daily to reduce bacteria levels and chance of disease.

Hiding places such as cork bark, halved coconut shells, or commercially manufactured caves are sold as additions to your cage, but are not necessarily the best choice for amphibians. Many of these products can get moldy and fall apart in humid environments, while others may have sharp edges that can harm the frog. Plants are also not a recommended decoration. Large Pacman frogs are heavy and will likely crush any type of live plants. A simple substrate and water dish setup is all you will need to raise a healthy frog. If you make the substrate deep enough for your frog to burrow under, you won't need to provide a hiding area—your frog will make his own.

Heating and Lighting for Juveniles

Once you have a cage and the substrate, you will need to create proper temperatures. These temperatures are for juvenile frogs, and we will discuss temperatures for adults later in this chapter. A

Although you have to change it each day, a substrate of damp papers towels is economical and safe for your frog.

Quick & Easy Horned Frog Care

All of the horned frogs, including the Surinam horned frog, like to burrow. To allow your frog to do so, you can use crushed coconut shells or sphagnum moss as a substrate.

heating pad or heat lamp will be necessary for juvenile horned frogs because they need a daytime temperature of 82-86°F. There are undertank heaters and overhead heat lamps available from most pet retailers. Undertank heaters work well and should create just enough heat for your frog. The heating pad should always be kept at one side of the cage, allowing for one side to be warmer than the other. This will allow the frog to control his own body temperature.

Heat lamps can sometimes dry out the air too quickly. You must keep a more watchful eye on temperatures and humidity if using overhead heat lamps.

Nighttime temperatures of 76-78°F will be tolerable for all species. You may need to get a thermostat or an additional nighttime heat lamp to accomplish this. Inexpensive thermostats are available today for more fail-proof temperature control.

Housing Your Horned Frog

A thermometer is a must. Do not rely on your perception to determine if the temperature is right. Digital thermometers are the most accurate and are usually available in electronics and department stores. The thermometer strips that stick on the side of the glass are often inaccurate.

Chacoan and other horned frogs will feed and grow best when they are kept at the proper temperature.

Light is not as important to these frogs as temperature. They do not need ultraviolet lighting, but lights can be added to make it easier to view your pet. Florescent lighting will illuminate the cage without disturbing the cage temperatures you have already set.

Caring for Your Juvenile Frog

When raising young frogs, the temperatures recommended above sustain a high metabolic rate, encouraging fast growth and reducing the possibility of your frog developing disease. At these temperatures, be sure to keep the enclosure adequately humidified, do not allow the water bowl to dry out, and make sure the substrate stays damp.

Raising Humidity

If you find the substrate in your frog's enclosure dries out too quickly, you can help maintain the humidity by covering half of the screen top. You can use a piece of glass or plastic food wrap. Be sure to only cover half of the screen, or you will reduce the air circulation too much.

Water Level

A good rule of thumb is to have the water level in your frog's bowl be no more than one-quarter the total height of your frog. This depth should allow your frog to exit and enter the bowl easily and prevent drowning.

Keeping the substrate and water bowl extremely clean is essential in the maintenance of your frog. When these frogs defecate and urinate, toxins build up and create an unsafe living environment. This means regular maintenance is critical. Make sure to change the water bowl daily and wash or change the bedding weekly. Also rinse the cage thoroughly to reduce the possibilities of any toxin build up.

Housing Adult Horned Frogs

Once horned frogs reach adulthood, you may find a different type of setup easier to maintain than the setup you used for your juvenile frog. In my experience, frogs who are three inches or larger in diameter do well with a substrate of pea-sized aquarium gravel with a shallow water dish sunken into the substrate. The gravel should be kept damp but not soaking wet.

The substrates that I mentioned earlier for keeping juvenile Pacman frogs will work fine for adults as well, but they require more maintenance and are not as simple as the pea-gravel method. Sphagnum or coconut husk needs to be replaced on a more regular basis with larger frogs, and you will not be able to reuse the same substrate over and over. With these types of substrate your frogs will probably bury themselves and you will not often see them. Each of these substrate has its pros and cons, but they will work fine for your frog. Choose the one that you find the most convenient.

Another good choice for a substrate is sphagnum moss. It holds humidity well and allows for burrowing.

Instead of using a water bowl, you can mold the gravel so that it slopes down, creating a water area and small shoreline. You will need to wash the gravel more often if this method is used, since you cannot simply remove the water dish and change the water. When choosing a water dish, you can use a clay plant saucer, a container lid, or one of the many realistic rock bowls that can be found in most pet stores. Just be sure to use a shallow one—only one-quarter to one-half an inch deep—so the frog can easily get in and out of it.

Be Careful With Gravel

If using a gravel substrate for larger frogs, be sure to feed your frog from forceps or slide a piece of cardboard under the frog's chin to prevent ingesting any gravel. Ingested gravel can block up the digestive track, a condition that is frequently fatal.

With adult frogs, temperatures can also be maintained a bit differently. Frogs three inches or larger can be safely maintained at 76-84°F with nighttime temperatures dropping into the low 70s. The same methods used to heat the juveniles can be applied here. Again, use a thermometer to monitor the temperature.

Keeping the enclosure clean is equally as important with adult frogs as with the juveniles. When using gravel for substrate, it should be washed every two weeks. This can be done by removing the gravel from the enclosure and rinsing it thoroughly in a bucket or sink. Rinse it several times until the water becomes mostly clean. The water dish should be changed daily as the adult frogs will tend to defecate in the water. These methods will work equally well for all species of horned frogs.

Handling Horned Frogs (or Not)

Most amphibians do not tolerate excessive handling. By handling them too much you jeopardize the protective coating that helps to protect the frog and hold in moisture. Also, amphibians have very thin and absorbent skin. Soap, perfume, and other things

If you house your horned frog on wet gravel, you must be careful that he does not ingest any gravel. You can do that by feeding him with forceps or by placing a piece of cardboard under his chin when feeding.

Can I Keep My Pacman Frogs Together?

Housing multiple horned frogs together is not usually a good idea. Although people have done this with some success, most have not. The safest situation is with adult frogs of similar size. In some cases, you can maintain similar-sized adults in the same enclosure, but it is risky. This is not recommended with younger animals that have more voracious appetites than the adults. If you are going to try to keep multiple Pacman frogs together, make sure they are equal in size; a larger one will surely consume a smaller one for lunch, dinner, or even a midday snack. Keeping each one in his own enclosure is best.

commonly found on human skin can be absorbed by your frog and prove to be detrimental to his health. When you do need to handle your frog, be sure your hands are free from chemicals, and only handle the frog with wet hands. Handle your frogs only when necessary; keep handling to a minimum. This will help to insure the frog's safety. Additionally, this will minimize the chances you will be bitten.

What Do Horned Frogs Eat?

All adult frogs are carnivorous, but different types of frogs eat different types of animals. Insects, fish, and even mammals are common prey for different types of frogs. Pacman frogs eat anything they can, as their name might suggest. Size and quantities of food for your new Argentine horned frog are also directly related to the age and size of the frog. Juvenile frogs can be fed a diet of crickets, fish, silkworms, mealworms, earthworms, and, if large enough, pink newborn mice. When raising a juvenile frog, be sure to maintain the higher temperatures we discussed earlier and to feed him several times a week. Feed appropriately sized meals; do not offer food that is too large for the frog to swallow. Horned frogs will attempt to eat

It is important to feed your horned frog appropriately sized prey. Although they can eat large meals, it is best to feed horned frogs prey that is half their size or smaller.

food that is too large for them to swallow. Make sure the food is about half the size of the frog. Feeding prey items that are too small may cause the frog to lose interest in eating, so this is not necessarily good either. It is very important to feed a varied diet. Too much of any one thing is not ideal for most herp pets.

Food Size Matters

Pacman frogs are famous for eating prey that is huge compared to their own size. Some keepers find it entertaining to feed their frogs a huge mouse or worm. However, it is best for your frog—especially when he is a juvenile—if you refrain from feeding giant meals. A good rule of thumb is to not feed your frog any prey items that are over half the size of the frog. That will prevent possible injuries or digestive problems caused by overly large meals.

Quick & Easy Horned Frog Care

Feeding Insects

Let's start with crickets. Crickets are a common food for reptiles and can be purchased from almost any pet retailer. If you are feeding crickets be sure to gut-load them. Gut-loading is a term used by herpers to describe the process of feeding your crickets or other feeder insects a highly nutritious diet so that they may pass those nutrients on to your pets. It ensures you are not feeding a hollow, unfulfilling diet to your frog. Crickets do not have high nutritional value if they have not been fed a good diet. Buy crickets from the store before you are ready to feed your frog and set them up in their own cage. Small plastic pet habitats make good cricket keepers. You will need to feed the crickets a nutritious diet for at least 24 hours prior to feeding them to your frogs. There are many commercial cricket diets available today from pet retailers. Also, be sure to give the crickets water or some vegetation to hydrate them. Carrots or the stems of leafy greens seem to work well, and they provide additional vitamins that will be passed on to your frog. If you decide to use a water dish for your crickets, make sure you put a sponge or

Frog-Eat-Frog World

It may surprise you, but quite a number of frogs feed heavily on other frogs. The horned frogs will try to eat anything that moves, including other frogs. One species of horned frog, the Surinam horned frog, *C. cornuta*, preys primarily on smaller frogs. This is one of the major reasons why Surinam horned frogs do so poorly in captivity. They often do not eat if not offered frogs, and if they do eat, they often fail to thrive on a non-frog diet.

The Brazilian horned frog, *C. aurita*, is thought to feed mainly on other frogs. However, little is known about the diet of this animal, so this may or may not be true. The question of the Brazilian horned frog's diet awaits further study.

Ceratophrys cornuta, *the Amazonian horned frog, is one of the species of horned frogs that preys primarily on other frogs in the wild.*

cotton in the water so the crickets do not get trapped in it and drown. You will need to clean the water dish frequently, because the crickets will mess it up. Once the crickets have consumed the food for a day or two they are ready to be fed to your frog.

Homemade Gut-Load

If you want to save some money or exercise more control over your crickets' diet, you can make your own gut-load. There are numerous recipes for gut-loads on the Internet.

A simple but nutritious gut-load can be made from equal parts rice baby cereal, whole oats, and wheat germ combined in a food processor with a pinch of reptile vitamin and mineral supplement. This will be an adequate gut-loading diet for crickets and mealworms. When used with crickets, remember to include a source of moisture.

Other insects that are commonly available are waxworms, silkworms, mealworms, super worms (also called king mealworms), and goliath horn worms. These worms give you more diet options for your pet. Silkworms are farmed commercially on large scale today and have excellent nutritional value; they also can be purchased at a small size and grown large enough to feed even an adult Pacman frog with a huge appetite. They can go from pinhead size to over two inches in length in less than month. Earthworms are also a good alternative; they have high levels of protein and vitamins. Super worms and mealworms are my least favorite choices, but I have known people who have had success feeding these types of prey. In my experience, frogs do not seem as interested in mealworms as they are in other types of food. Also, mealworms tend to drown quickly, so if your frog doesn't eat them right away, they will go to waste.

Feeding wild insects is also an option. If you have the ambition to catch wild insects, these bugs will make welcome snacks for your

Ornate and other horned frogs lack teeth on the mandible, but they have an odontoid, a ridge of sharp bone that serves the same function as teeth.

What Do Horned Frogs Eat?

frogs. Do not ever use wild insects if you have any reason to believe they have come in contact with insecticides. This could be fatal to your frog. Wild insects can add variety to the diets of your herps. If you go out collecting feeder insects, you must become familiar with any toxic or dangerous insects that may live in your area.

Feeding Fish and Rodents

Because horned frogs are so voracious and get so large, you are not limited to feeding these frogs insects. In fact, most keepers feed their frogs some type of vertebrate prey, usually either fish or mice. Both of these food items are available at most pet stores.

Several sizes of feeder fish are normally available at pet stores. Guppies are the smallest and can be used to feed small horned frogs. Minnows or rosy reds are bigger than guppies and can be used to feed larger juveniles, while feeder goldfish and larger whole fish can be fed to the adults. Mice are available in a similar range of sizes: pinkies (so-called because they are pink and hairless), fuzzies (baby

Earthworms can be purchased or collected from a chemical-free yard. They are a nutritious item to feed horned frogs, such as this fantasy frog.

Various feeder fish should be available at your local pet store. To avoid a thi-amin deficiency, feed live or freshly killed fish instead of frozen ones.

mice that have grown fur), hoppers (older young mice that are big enough to hop around), and adults. Pinkies are generally too big for froglets, but they can be fed to good-sized juveniles.

If you are feeding fish, or your frog is large enough to consume pink mice, there is less need for supplementation than if you are feeding insects (see below for information on vitamin supplements). This diet is more complete because you are feeding a whole animal, including the bones and organs. Digesting the bones provide your frog high levels of calcium, essential for bone development.

Feeder rosies or goldfish have worked very well for me in raising Pacman frogs. This diet seems to build them up to rodent-eating size quickly. Some herpers have speculated that feeding fish with high levels of thiaminase, such as goldfish, can cause vitamin B deficiencies and lead to possible neurological disorders. At this time,

Fantasy frogs and most other horned frogs get large enough to eat mice and other sizable prey.

there have been no long-term studies that address this concern. I have fed feeder fish as a base diet and have seen no ill effects. Vitamin B deficiencies in herps seem to occur most often in those animals fed a lot of frozen fish.

Contrary to popular belief, you do not have to feed rodents to Pacman frogs, although rodents do provide a complete and well-rounded diet. Pacman frogs can be raised on fish and worms, if you so desire.

Calcium and Vitamin Supplementation

Calcium is a critical part of your horned frog's diet. These stocky frogs have large skulls and big bones, and bones are primarily composed of calcium. In the early stages of development, horned frogs need a great quantity of calcium in order for these large bones to grow and develop properly. If you are feeding a diet of crickets, it is essential to gut-load and supplement the crickets with a good quality calcium supplement that includes vitamin D3. Vitamin D3 is responsible for the proper metabolism of calcium. If enough calcium is not absorbed, deficiencies develop that can cause deformities and even death. This calcium deficiency is called metabolic bone disease or MBD. This condition is noticeable in Pacman frogs in several ways. One of the easiest symptoms to notice are deformities of the jaws and possibly squishy soft face. The bottom jaw will often hang down or turn outward. This is commonly called rubber jaw and is the result of inadequate calcium in the bones of the jaws and face. Another common physical characteristic of MBD is the frog's legs being unable to support his weight. This happens because the legs are soft and splay out to the sides. Both of these symptoms are easy to diagnose. With a change in diet and proper supplementation, these conditions can be halted and sometimes reversed. If MBD is allowed to progress too far, the bone deformities will become permanent and more severe.

Baby horned frogs grow rapidly and need plenty of calcium to properly form the heavy bones of the legs and skull.

What Do Horned Frogs Eat?

If you are feeding mostly insects, you should include a good calcium and vitamin supplement into your frog's diet every second or third feeding. If you are feeding rodents and fish, you do not need to supplement more than once or twice a month.

Most supplements are in powdered form and can be added to almost any food source. There are several good quality calcium and vitamin supplements available at most pet shops. Be sure to use a vitamin and mineral supplement that is made specifically for herps. Also, use one that has at least twice as much calcium as phosphorus, which will interfere with absorption of calcium.

Feeding Your Frog Throughout His life

As your frog grows, his food sources should grow also. Feed larger prey as the frog gets bigger, but always stick to the half-the-body size prey rule. From crickets, rosies, and goldfish you can move to pink mice, then fuzzy mice, and on to adult mice. An adult Pacman frog can easily consume an adult mouse. As your frog matures, you will

My Pacman Frog Won't Eat

If your Pacman frog stops eating in the winter, don't be too alarmed. Cooler house temperatures may stimulate your frog to enter a hibernation period. This would be your frog's normal response to low temperatures in the wild. If your frog is less active and does not eat but otherwise seems fine—in other words, not losing weight or showing other signs of illness—do not worry. This is a common phenomena, and as the seasons change the frog will regain his normal appetite.

You can reverse this in some cases by increasing the ambient air temperature and tricking the frog into thinking it is spring or summer again. This is not necessary, but some keepers would rather have the animal feeding year round.

Quick & Easy Horned Frog Care

Frogs do not drink. Instead, they absorb water through their skin. Because your frog directly absorbs the water in his terrarium, you must keep the water extremely clean.

need to feed him less frequently. When he is about a year old, you can cut back your feeding schedule to about once a week, rather than the several times a week you were feeding him as a juvenile. When your frog reaches about two years old, feeding once every 10 to 14 days will maintain his proper weight and body condition. Always watch your frog's weight and feed accordingly. If you notice the frog does not have a nice fat appearance and his hip bones begin to show, feed more frequently. However, if your frog becomes so bloated that you can not see his legs, feed less often or smaller prey items. The amount of food somewhat depends on the individual frog.

For horned frogs, presentation of the food source sometimes makes a difference. If you are feeding dead or pre-killed foods, acquire a pair of forceps or hemostats to hold the food and present it to the frog. Sometimes moving the food around on the end of the forceps will make it much more appealing. This type of interaction also makes the frog a more entertaining pet.

What Do Horned Frogs Eat?

Do Frogs Drink?

This may seem like an odd question, but the answer may surprise you. Frogs do not drink like many of our other pets do. Horned frogs absorb water through their belly skin. They also take in water through their vent, which then moves up into the bladder. This water that enters the frogs body is the same water that is in the water dish in the enclosure, making it critical to keep the water very clean. When your frog eliminates in his water, the toxins and bacteria make the water unsafe for him. Clearly, you must change the water on a daily basis.

Tap water is fine for your frogs, but just check with your local water company to make sure they are not adding chlorine or chloramines to purify the water for drinking. These chemicals are safe for humans to consume but can be harmful to your frogs. If these chemicals are in your water, go to your local pet retailer and purchase a chlorine and chloramine remover. There are many available for just this purpose. Bottled drinking water is also safe, but do not use distilled or purified water. Because distilled water is pure water with no minerals, it can interfere with your frog's internal ion balance, possibly killing him.

Breeding Your Horned Frogs

Captive breeding by both hobbyists and professional breeders is a very important source of the reptile and amphibian pets that we all know and love. While many animals are still collected from the wild, increasingly captive breeding is providing the animals for the hobby. This is a good trend, since collecting of most species can not go on forever. The wild populations of many species of herps are declining—usually more through habitat loss than collecting from the pet trade—so continuing to collect them for the pet trade may help push the animals toward extinction.

Note that the throat of this huge ornate horned frog has a slightly blue coloration. This is one clue that this individual is probably male.

Frogs are not necessarily one of the easiest animals to reproduce in captivity, but today it is happening with more and more success. In this chapter, I will try to outline some techniques for reproducing Argentine horned frogs in captivity. These methods have been successful in the past and are being used to commercially raise some of these frogs today. If you intend on trying to breed your frogs, make sure you have the right motivation. A successful breeding of these frogs may be too much for many people to deal with; most people are not able to care for hundreds of tadpoles and froglets. If you would like to try it, don't mind a good deal of work, and have somewhere to place the babies, then this may be right for you.

Getting Started

The first step in breeding any animal is determining whether or not you have a mature, sexable pair who are healthy and vigorous. Adult males are much smaller in size than females and usually have a dark colored throat. Males will also vocalize at night when in breeding condition. The call of the Argentine horned frog sounds much like a cow mooing. Spraying them with water will often encourage them to vocalize. Never attempt to breed underweight frogs or frogs that are not 100 percent healthy.

Once you have determined that you have at least one pair, you are ready to start the process. In the wild, horned frogs breed when the rains start after a dry, cool period during which they lay dormant for one to two months. They bury themselves into the ground and do not eat during this time. In captivity, it is necessary to put the frogs through this natural cooling process to prepare them for breeding. A good method to do this is to set up a new cage for the hibernation period. A 10-gallon aquarium with sphagnum moss or coconut husk is the best setup; the frog can burrow into the substrate. The bedding can be slightly damp to begin the process, but do not moisten it as you normally would. Do not mist the substrate during this period; maintain a drier environment than usual. A water bowl should always be accessible to prevent the frog from dehydrating if necessary. During this period, temperatures should be reduced to 65 to 70°F and remain in that range for about two months. This is around the normal room temperatures for an average household, so probably will not need any heating devices. Usually the frogs will not eat during this period, so there is no need to offer any food to them.

Hold the Hormones

For many years, it was believed that to breed Pacman frogs you needed to inject the adult frogs with LHRH, a pituitary stimulating hormone. However, this technique was dangerous and sometimes killed the frogs.

Now that the conditions to stimulate the frogs to breed are better understood, most breeders produce horned frogs without resorting to drugs.

Chacoan horned frogs breed in this pool in northwestern Paraguay. Breeding in this and most horned frog species commences after the rainy season begins.

Let It Rain

After the cooling process, you will need to set them up in an aquarium or plastic tub with shallow water. This tub will serve as a rain chamber for your frogs. The water should be just deep enough for the frogs to touch the bottom. The water should be about the same temperature that you would keep horned frogs at normally—76 to 84°F.

Once you have the rain chamber set up and at the proper temperature, you must simulate a rainy season. This can be accomplished in several different ways. The least expensive and easiest method would be to use a pump-up misting sprayer and spray your frogs several times a day. These misting sprayers can be purchased at garden centers and home improvement stores. Be sure to purchase ones that do not contain any chemicals and are for misting plants with water only. If you are very serious about breeding these frogs, commercial misting systems are available but can be rather pricy. Rain chambers can also be created with aquarium pumps and filters.

Quick & Easy Horned Frog Care

Misters

A variety of handheld misters are available at gardening and home improvement stores. They range from simple and inexpensive varieties to larger and more expensive ones. The types that allow you generate a constant mist without continuous pumping will be more comfortable for you use and definitely worth the money.

Stationary misters with timers are useful for creating rain chambers. They tend to be much more expensive than the handheld type. If you are getting into frog breeding on more than a casual level, they will save you a lot of time and effort. You can find them at herp expos, online, and possibly at herp-oriented pet stores.

One type of rain chamber can be created by using a 30- to 55-gallon aquarium that is equipped with a bottom drain. A valve will have to be installed to allow the water to slowly drain into a bucket. In the drainage bucket, you will need a submersible pump or aquarium filter to pick the water up and return it to the tank. The valves should be adjusted to keep 1/2 to 1 inch of water at the bottom of the aquarium at all times. When the water is

Different Calls for Different Frogs

The calls of male frogs attract the females to mate. Each species of frog has a unique call that the female can readily identify. The calls are very specific. In fact, there are species of frogs that look identical to the human eye but have different calls. The females of each species never mate with the other species. Scientists determined this by analyzing the genes of frogs from many populations. This research led to the realization that the common gray tree frog of North America was actually two species with different calls and gene pools but with an externally identical appearance.

returned to the tank via the pump or filter, it should then be channeled though a spray bar that can be made of PVC piping with small holes drilled in it allowing the water to trickle or rain out of it. Mount the spray bar over the top of the tank. This raining should be set up to happen several times a day for several minutes at each time. During this time—and with any luck—breeding should occur.

Be sure to have a drain so the water does not become too deep and drown the frogs. Set up your rain chamber to rain on your frogs in the evening for a few days straight until you see breeding and then egg laying. Once the frogs have bred, the raining can cease. If you are using a single male, you can encourage him to breed by recording his vocalization and playing it back so he thinks there are other males trying to breed with his female.

You should include some aquatic plants to give the frogs a place to attach their eggs. Plants that will work well are anacharis,

Like typical frogs, ornate horned lay eggs in water that hatch into tadpoles. The tadpoles eventually develop legs and leave the water to live on land.

Horned frog tadpoles can be individually reared in deli cups or other small containers. While this is labor-intensive for the breeder, it cuts down on cannibalism among the tadpoles.

cabomba, and hornwort; you can purchase aquatic plants at most tropical fish retailers. Egg laying typically occurs three to five days after the simulated rainy season begins. Once the eggs are laid, remove the frogs from the tank and return them to their normal setups. A normal healthy breeding will yield 1,000 to 2,000 eggs. After you remove the adults, double the volume of water in the aquarium, and the eggs should begin to hatch in two to four days.

Caring for Tadpoles

Once tadpoles have emerged from the eggs you can use one of two methods to raise them. One is to separate each tadpole into its own small enclosure. This method is very time consuming and labor intensive and not very practical. The second method is to raise all of the tadpoles together in a large tub or tank. This method is more practical but will produce fewer froglets, as the tadpoles are cannibalistic. If you are raising them together, it is best to include many live or artificial plants, so the tadpoles can hide from each other. This will cut down on the cannibalism. The water should be filtered with a small sponge filter or changed daily. One breeding can yield up to 1,500 tadpoles, so you can see how the individual cage method is not practical, unless you can devote most of your time to caring for tadpoles.

Horned frog tadpoles are aggressive feeders and do well feeding on a diet of live tubifex or black worms. These are common live fish foods and can be purchased at many pet stores. They may also eat freeze-dried kill and other similar items. Feed the tadpoles once a day.

The water should be heated to 78 to 86°F. The warmer the temperature of the water, the faster the tadpoles will grow and metamorphose into frogs. If you maintain temperatures on the cooler side, you will rear larger, stronger frogs but it will take a bit longer for them to come out of the water. If all goes well, you should have frogs within three to five weeks. After the third week you will need to provide some sort of land area so the emerging froglets can seek safety out of the water.

Caring for Froglets

Once your frogs are out of the water, you will need to make another decision: keep each newly changed (or *morphed* in herper lingo) froglet separate or keep them in a large group together. As with the

Once the tadpoles develop legs, you must provide then with a way to leave the water. Otherwise, the froglets will drown.

This juvenile Amazonian horned frog has only recently left the water. Note that he still has a small stub of a tail.

tadpoles, keeping them together runs the risk of cannibalism. Baby horned frogs are voracious feeders, and you may find frogs being consumed by other frogs on a daily basis. If you are very ambitious and are interested in the greatest yield from your breeding, you could choose to house each froglet individually in his own small plastic cup. Eight-ounce deli cups with holes punched in them and a tight-fitting lid will do the trick. You could use taller plastic cups that the frogs cannot jump out of for a lidless setup. The water should be cleaned on a daily basis to keep the frogs from making the water toxic.

Baby Pacman frogs are very easy to feed. If there is one thing we can assume they love, it is eating. Baby frogs usually begin to feed after their tails have been fully absorbed. Once you see no remnants of the tail, you can begin to feed the baby frogs. Baby Pacman frogs basically eat anything that moves. Small goldfish, rosy reds, guppies, crickets, mealworms, and—if you are not careful—your fingers! All

Breeding Your Horned Frogs

but your fingers are good choices to start the feeding of your baby frogs. As they grow, you should care for them just as we outlined in the previous chapters.

This whole process seems like a great deal of work, and make no mistake, it is. This project will cost you more time than money, but if you are serious about raising frogs, it will be well worth it.

Horned Frog Health Care

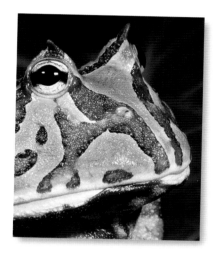

Although the common species of horned frogs are hardy pets, there is a small possibility that one can become sick. I will outline the most common ailments that may creep up to prepare you for the unlikely. If you maintain your frog under the most ideal conditions, it will greatly reduce the possibility of having any problems. Good husbandry is the key to success when caring for any type of amphibian.

If you notice a problem, you should seek veterinary care. Although some minor problems can be treated by a knowledgeable hobbyist, it is best for your frog to have veterinary input. Search your local vet hospitals as well as the Internet and

Finding a Herp Vet

It is not always easy to find vets who are experienced with reptiles and amphibians. In rural areas, it may be impossible to find one within a reasonable distance. Here are some suggestions to help you locate a vet who can help with your frog. It is best if you locate one before you actually have an emergency

- Call veterinarians listed as "exotic" or "reptile" vets in the phonebook. Ask them questions to be sure they are familiar with horned frogs.
- Ask at your local pet stores and animal shelters to see if there is someone they can recommend.
- Ask local zoos and animal shelters for a recommendation.
- Herp societies are likely to know which vets treat reptiles and amphibians.
- Contact the Association of Reptilian and Amphibian Veterinarians. Their website is www.arav.org.

try to locate a reputable and knowledgeable exotic vet that has experience with reptiles and amphibians. This is sometimes not an easy task, and it is a good idea to do this research before you have an actual problem. Some common problems that occur with horned frogs in captivity are outlined in this chapter. This does not mean everyone can diagnose every problem, so if you have any doubt, consult a vet.

Intestinal Blockage

Blockages of the digestive tract are usually caused by your frog swallowing substrate. Gravel and some other types of substrate can cause blockages if consumed. You can prevent this from happening by feeding the frog from hemostats or forceps and watching to make sure no bedding is ingested. Another method that has worked for me is to slide a thin piece of cardboard under the chin of the frog just prior to feeding. The cardboard keeps the frog's mouth away from the substrate as the frog is lunging for the food.

If your frog stops eating suddenly, vomits, or passes blood from the vent, you should suspect a blockage. Treat this condition as an emergency, as it can prove fatal. You should contact your vet immediately. It is likely that your frog will need surgery.

Red Leg

The infection known as red leg is generally a direct result of inadequate husbandry. Unsanitary conditions cause bacteria to become more numerous, allowing the bacteria more of an opportunity to infect your frog. Additionally, stress can weaken a frog's immune system, allowing these organisms to overwhelm his defenses.

The most common symptom is red coloration on the underside of the belly and legs, caused by the rupture of capillaries. Other symptoms include listlessness, partial skin sloughing, and cloudy

Chacoan and other horned frogs grow fast, taking only a little more than a year to reach adult size.

Keeping your horned frog in a dirty cage will make him prone to red leg and other serious ailments. Good hygiene is important for the health of your frog.

eyes. Red leg is the common name for a bacterial septicemia that causes high mortality in frogs. Commonly implicated pathogens are *Aeromonas hydrophila, Proteus hydrophilus,* and *Pseudomonas hydrophilus.* These are by no means the only organisms that can cause this disease, but they among the most common ones associated with it.

Treatment can be done with certain antibiotic medications, but the success rate is not good. You will need to consult a veterinarian for the medication. When treating, it is important to maintain the frog at a slightly higher temperature. This allows the frog's immune system to work more efficiently. Raise the temperature about five degrees above the normal keeping temperatures.

Toxing Out

Another common ailment is something herpers refer to as "toxing out" or "toxing out syndrome." It is another ailment caused by poor

Quick & Easy Horned Frog Care

keeping conditions. When a frog's substrate and water are not changed frequently, the toxins that almost all frogs produce build up—along with waste products and bacteria—in the captive environment. Eventually, the levels of all these poisons reach a threshold that threatens the life of your frog. In many cases this problem will creep up so fast it is nearly impossible to cure. If this if what is wrong with your frog, you will notice that the frog will become increasingly uncomfortable and start bouncing around the cage much more than normal. Occasionally the eyes will become cloudy or opaque from the stress, and you may notice muscle tremors and spasms. If you see any of these things occur, change the water and substrate immediately. Cleaning up the environment so the frog can flush the toxins from its system is his only hope. If you are too late, the legs will usually spasm just prior to the frog expiring.

When using potting soil, moss, or crushed coconut shell as your horned frog's substrate, remember to change it as needed to prevent a build up of toxins.

Horned Frog Health Care

Keep Your Frog From Flipping Over

It is important to make sure your Pacman frog does not get himself stuck upside down. With their short legs, larger Pacman frogs can not always flip themselves over and can possibly drown when stuck in this upside down position. Babies have a much easier time getting themselves upright than adults do, so you normally don't have to be concerned with this problem when your horned frog is a baby. When housing adults, avoid including too much cage furniture that could flipped a horned frog over.

Edema

Edema is another ailment sometimes associated with Pacman frogs. As with the other problems that commonly occur, this one is also typically a direct result of poor husbandry practices. If the frog is kept over a period of time in less than desirable conditions, liver and kidney damage can occur from absorbing high levels of toxins, making this problem similar to toxing out. Water edema can be spotted easily, as the horned frog appears overly bloated. The body, as well as the limbs, retain large quantities of water as a result of impaired kidney function.

If you notice any swelling, keep the frog in a dry environment until the swelling subsides. Many times it is already too late for your poor frog once you notice the problem. The hidden damage to the filtering organs will cause the frog to die within the next few months.

It is thought that overfeeding could also be the culprit in this problem, but it is more likely that maintaining the animal in toxic conditions is the more common cause. Keeping clean water and ideal conditions can make this fatal disease unlikely to strike your frog.

Skin Sloughing

This problem is seen in both adult frogs and tadpoles. The most visible symptom is the skin sloughing off the frog, but it is not primarily a disease of the skin. It is rather the coating of the frog's skin being thrown off due to excessive stress. Cloudy eyes, listlessness, and bloating are also common symptoms that go along with this problem. Some breeders believe this to be contagious, so be sure to keep frogs or tadpoles exhibiting any of these signs separated from others. Medicating with certain antibiotics has been effective in a few cases. Some have suggested that nitrofurizone (an antibiotic fish medication that can be purchased at most pet stores) at two times the normal strength for medicating tropical fish is the best medication. Consult a herp veterinarian before medicating.

If your juvenile horned frog is not getting enough calcium in his diet, he will get metabolic bone disease, a condition similar to the human disease rickets.

Metabolic Bone Disease

The last (but not least) possible problem to be aware of is metabolic bone disease, or MBD. MBD is a disease that is a direct result of a lack of calcium for bone growth. Calcium and vitamin D3 are vital in the skeletal development of the frog. Argentine horned frogs have massive skeletons with very large skulls. This big frame needs a great amount of calcium and vitamin D3 for its bones to develop properly. Coupled with its larger-than-its-eyes appetite and high rate of growth, they need adequate levels of calcium is essential. If fed a diet that does not provide enough calcium, metabolic bone disease can result. The early symptoms of MBD are rubber jaw or rear leg mobility loss. If you notice your frog hanging its mouth open or you can push in his nose, he may have the start of MBD. If its rear legs splay out behind it, it may not be getting enough calcium for its bones to grow properly. If feeding insects, be sure to gut-load them to insure proper nutrition. Giving your frog calcium supplements or feeding him a calcium-rich diet can help to reverse or prevent this disease. See the feeding chapter for the details of a proper diet.

Types of Horned Frogs and Related Species

The popularity of Argentine horned frogs, along with the growth in the herp hobby in general, has created a market for other frogs requiring similar care and of similar size and impressiveness. The herp community is always interested in some new species or color varieties. In today's market, there are many more frogs offered than when the horned frogs first hit the herp scene in the early 1980s. Now we see hybrid frogs, albino frogs, and other related species in the pet shops and at the herp shows. This chapter looks at some different species you may see offered for sale from time to time. These are all species related to the Chacoan and Ornate horned frogs. The family Ceratophryidae is composed of the genera *Ceratophrys*, the horned frogs, *Chacophrys*, a horned frog-like species that has been becoming more and more available to hobbyists, and *Lepidobatrachus*, the Budgett's frogs.

Horned Frog Species

Chacoan Horned Frog

The Chacoan or Argentine horned frog, *Ceratophrys cranwelli*, probably is the most popular horned frog in the hobby. These frogs are originally from the Chacoan region of South America, an area containing parts of Argentina, Bolivia, Brazil, and Paraguay. They are similar to the ornate horned frog, but have slightly different markings and color and seem to have a larger head that is a bit more set off from the body. They are commonly offered today in a variety of different colors.

The first people to reproduce this frog in captivity were Robert Mailloux and Phillippe de Vosjoli, paving the way for this frog to become the mainstay of the herp industry it is today. Through commercial captive breeding, these frogs are now available in large numbers to the general public. There is a bright green color variation—a direct result of this sort of selective captive breeding—offered under the common name of green Pacman frog. The other common color is brown, which may at first not seem very appealing, but I can tell you from experience that given some time, these frogs turn into exceptional looking adults. Some acquire oranges and yellows as they mature and are quite attractive. These are known throughout the pet industry as brown Pacman frogs.

Along with these two color variations is an albino form. This frog was first developed in 1992 by Kim Thomas of The Frog Ranch and is now a staple in most pet stores around the country and quite possibly the world. It is a bright yellow and orange frog with pinkish eyes who turns into an awesome animal as an adult. They are commonly sold under the name albino Pacman frog.

Amazonian Horned Frog

The Amazonian horned frog, *Ceratorphrys cornuta*, is also known as the Surinam horned frog. This frog is still imported with some regularity and captive bred by some hobbyists but is not a readily available species. Two factors have prevented this frog from being more popular in the hobby. First, it seems the imported specimens, who commonly come in from Guyana and Surinam, have heavy parasite loads. Unlike many wild caught reptiles, these frogs do not always tolerate deworming medication. Their digestive and immune systems seem more fragile and less tolerant of outside agents. The second thing that seems to hold them back is their diet. In the wild, they primarily eat other frogs. In captivity, it is not very practical to feed frogs to other frogs, and it makes this species very hard to acclimate. In my experience, I have been able to acquire captive-bred specimens who were parasite free and easier to feed, having already been acclimated to captive environments.

This species has some of the most defined horns atop its head, making it a very impressive and desirable frog to keep. Their care is generally similar to Chacoan horned frogs with the exception that this frog needs a slightly higher temperature. Daytime temps of 78 to 85°F are preferred by this species. If you are thinking of keeping this species, it is best to try to acquire a captive-bred specimen. This will give you a much greater chance of success than you would have working with an imported frog.

The Amazonian (or Surinam) horned frog has the largest horns of the group. Unfortunately, they usually fail to adapt to captivity.

Fantasy Frog

The fantasy frog is one of the most impressive horned frogs you can get. Available at pet

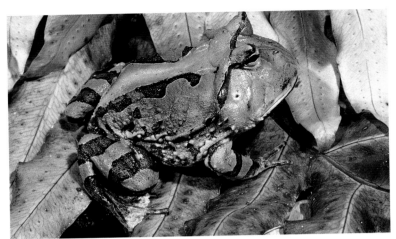

Amazonian horned frogs also occur in a green phase. As the captive breeding of this species becomes more common, selection for brighter colors is sure to occur.

stores from time to time, you may be able to acquire one of these unique horned frogs. The fantasy frog is a man-made hybrid between the two aforementioned species, the Chacoan horned frog and the Amazonian horned frog. Breeding these two frogs together makes an outstanding, colorful hybrid.

This frog is the best of two worlds. He has the appetite and simple care of the Chacoan and the pronounced horns and variety of colors of the Amazonian. These frogs are very hardy eaters and feed much more easily than Amazonian horned frogs. The colors are outstanding—from bright lime green with intricate dorsal patterning to bright pink with the same dorsal striping as the Amazonian. These frogs also seem to reach a much larger size than either of

The fantasy frog (green) is a hybrid between a Chacoan horned frog and an Amazonian horned frog (brown). Fantasy frogs themselves are sterile.

Quick & Easy Horned Frog Care

their parents. I personally have seen seven-inch specimens of this hybrid.

This frog can be kept with the same care and housing as the Argentine but sometimes takes up to two years to reach full size. If you are interested in breeding fantasy frogs, you will need to get a Chacoan and an Ama-

Ceratophrys aurita, *the Brazilian horned frog, is an impressive amphibian similar in appearance to* C. cornuta.

zonian to make this hybrid yourself. These frogs are mules and do not breed true. Generally, these frogs will be more expensive than other species due to the amount of work involved in creating this frog.

Some Rare Horned Frogs

Rarely seen in captivity are the giant Brazilian horned frogs, *Ceratophrys aurita*. These frogs inhabit Minas Gerais and Bahia to Rio Grande do Sul in Brazil. These frogs have extremely pronounced horns and grow to a huge size. Females of this species are said to reach nearly ten inches. The color is generally a dark green base similar to ornate horned frogs. The chances of this frog being offered in the reptile industry are slim unless Brazil changes its laws banning exportation. At this point in time, that does not seem likely, and keeping this frog is only a dream for breeders and serious herp hobbyists.

The Colombian horned frog, *Ceratophrys calcarata*, is yet another species not readily offered for sale. This is a much smaller species of horned frog that was once imported in large numbers. However, Colombia has changed its laws of exportation, and this frog is seldom offered for sale. This species only reaches an adult size just shy of three inches and doesn't have overly pronounced horns. On rare occasions, captive-bred specimens of these frogs are offered for sale but tend to require a

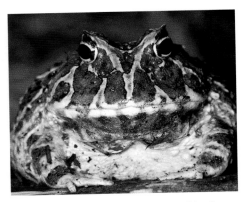

This Colombian horned frog has a bluish throat, indicating he is probably male. Colombian horned frogs are captive-bred in small numbers and are rare in the hobby.

specific diet. They seem to more easily feed on insects such as crickets and mealworms than on fish or pinkies.

The Joazeiro horned frog, *Ceratophrys joazeirensis*, is a horned frog that is found in a small locale. It comes from Joazeiro, Estado de Bahia, in Brazil. Little is known about this frog but it has many similar characteristics to *Ceratophrys cranwelli*.

The Peruvian horned frog, *Ceratophrys stolzmanni*, is another frog that is not offered in the herp marketplace. This is a nearly hornless species of horned frog and could be the most uncommon of them all. Specimens of this frog are not even known to exist in museums around the world. Little is known about this species except that they occur in extremely dry habitats of Peru and near the Gulf of Ecuador.

One of the smallest horned frogs, Colombian horned frogs need to be fed small food, such as insects and earthworms. The do not get big enough to eat rodents.

Other Hybrids

Other man-made frogs have been created, but none have been so warmly accepted and kept as the fantasy frog. The fantasy frog is the most impressive and readily available hybrid. Other hybrids include the Chacoan horned frog crossed with the Ornate horned frog (*Ceratophrys cranwelli* x *C. ornata*). This frog sometimes grows quite large and has interesting patterns. However, this hybrid is not often offered for sale. Another hybridized form is the Amazonian horned frog crossed with the Ornate horned frog (*C. cornuta* x *C. ornata*). This hybrid is the most difficult to produce. It seems many of the tadpoles do not survive to develop into froglets. The few that have made it have very bumpy

At this time, it does not seem anyone has successfully captive bred Chacophrys. *All those offered for sale are wild-caught.*

Budgett's frogs frequently prey on other frogs in the wild. This Paraguayan Budgett's frog is eating a termite frog, Dermatonotus muelleri.

Budgett's frogs can be aggressive and have a bad bite; note the fang-like odontoid on the bottom jaw. Handling these amphibians is not advised.

Types of Horned Frogs and Related Species 59

skin and average-size horns. A great deal of red coloring is evident as is a large number of spots on the body. This particular hybrid is also not commonly offered for sale.

Chacophrys

Another interesting frog is *Chacophrys pierrotti*. This is a smaller species of frog that looks much like a horned frog. It is a rounded, almost spherical frog with no horns. The color is dark green with two wide, lighter green stripes. It is more readily available now than in years past, but still, little is known about this frog. It was once thought to be a naturally occurring hybrid between a Chacoan horned frog and a Budgett's frog (*Ceratophrys cranwelli* x *Lepidobatrachus llanensis*). I have personally kept this frog; maintaining them under the same conditions of horned frogs seems to work well. In my experience, a diet of insects was preferred over other foods. Unlike the tadpoles of horned frogs, *Chacophrys* tadpoles are vegetarian.

Budgett's Frogs

Horned frogs are related to some very interesting characters. The Budgett's frogs are large brownish-grey frogs with smooth skin,

Young Budgett's frog (L. asper pictured here) are quite colorful. However, the adults are generally drab gray, cream, and brown.

Name Game

round bodies, and tiny little eyes with vertical pupils. Their beady eyes and big round bodies somewhat resemble a cartoon character, and it is hard to believe this is a living creature. Budgett's frogs also come from South America, specifically from the Gran Chaco Region that includes parts of Argentina, Paraguay, and Brazil. Freddie Krueger frogs, as they are sometimes referred to in the pet trade, make quite interesting pets. Freddie Krueger, as some of you may know, is the scary villain of the *Nightmare on Elm Street* movies. The way the frog snarls, growls, and lunges at you with open mouth gave him this nickname.

Their care is similar to their cousins, the Pacman frogs, with the exception that they prefer slightly deeper water. Their feet are better adapted for burrowing and swimming than jumping. Budgett's are a bit more aquatic than horned frogs and spend more time in the water. These frogs are best kept under similar conditions to Pacman frogs, but with a half-land, half-water type setup. Feeding is essentially the same and common food sources that work well are crickets, fish, and small rodents. Adult Budgett's frogs can easily feed on adult mice.

There are three recognized species of Budgett's frogs. *Lepidobatrachus llanensis*, or the dwarf Budgett's frog (sometimes called the llanos Budgett's frog), is available in the pet trade on occasion. This species only reaches adult sizes of two to three inches—a fairly manageable size. If you are looking for a larger frog similar to the ultimate size of a Pacman frog, you may want to choose *Lepidobatrachus laevis*. This is the true Budgett's frog and reaches a size of nearly seven inches. They are

Dwarf Budgett's frogs reach an adult size of just over three inches. They are not as common in the hobby as the true Budgett's frog.

reproduced in fairly large numbers and are commonly available for sale. They are large, aggressive frogs with huge appetites and are not opposed to making their owner's fingers a choice for lunch. The third species is *Lepidobatrachus asper*, sometimes called the Paraguayan Budgett's frog. There is some debate of whether this is a valid species. Some breeders have bred *laevis* to *llanensis* and produced a frog very similar to, if not the same, as *Lepidobatrachus asper*. This has led some people to believe asper is a natural occurring hybrid between *laevis* and *llanensis*. This hybrid frog is also one that is offered on a small scale to the pet trade and is the one commonly called the Freddie Krueger frog. *L. asper* is usually not offered for sale, but this hybrid (which seems to be essentially the same frog) sometimes is.

Quick & Easy Horned Frog Care

Resources

MAGAZINES

Reptiles Magazine
P.O. Box 6050
Mission Viejo, CA 92690
www.animalnetwork.com/reptiles

Contemporary Herpetology
Southeastern Louisiana University
www.nhm.ac.uk/hosted_sites/ch

Herp Digest
www.herpdigest.org

ORGANIZATIONS

American Society of Ichthyologists and Herpetologists
Maureen Donnelly, Secretary
Grice Marine Laboratory
Florida International University
Biological Sciences
11200 SW 8th St.
Miami, FL 33199
Telephone: (305) 348-1235
E-mail: asih@fiu.edu
www.asih.org

Society for the Study of Amphibians and Reptiles (SSAR)
Marion Preest, Secretary
The Claremont Colleges
925 N. Mills Ave.
Claremont, CA 91711
Phone: 909-607-8014
E-mail: mpreest@jsd.claremont.edu
www.ssarherps.org

Amphibian, Reptile & Insect Association
Liz Price
23 Windmill Rd
Irthlingsborough
Wellingborough NN9 5RJ
England

List of Local Herp Societies
www.kingsnake.com/society.html

WEB RESOURCES

Frogdaze
www.frogdaze.com

Frog Directory
www.frogdirectory.com

Frogland
www.allaboutfrogs.org

Living Under World
www.livingunderworld.org

Kingsnake
www.kingsnake.com

Kingsnake (UK)
www.kingsnake.co.uk

HerpNetwork
www.herpnetwork.com

VETERINARY RESOURCES

Association of Reptile and Amphibian Veterinarians
P.O. Box 605
Chester Heights, PA 19017
Phone: 610-358-9530
Fax: 610-892-4813
E-mail: ARAVETS@aol.com
www.arav.org

RESCUE AND ADOPTION SERVICES

ASPCA
424 East 92nd Street
New York, NY 10128-6801
Phone: (212) 876-7700
E-mail: information@aspca.org
www.aspca.org

RSPCA (UK)
Wilberforce Way
Southwater
Horsham, West Sussex RH13 9RS
Telephone: 0870 3335 999
www.rspca.org.uk

Index

Measurement Conversion Chart

UNITS USED IN THIS BOOK
1 gallon = 3.7854 liters
1 inch = 2.54 centimeters
32°F = 0°C (water freezes)
75°F = 23.9°C

CONVERTING FAHRENHEIT TO CELSIUS
Subtract 32 from the Fahrenheit temperature.
Divide the answer by 9.
Multiply that answer by 5.